LITANIES
NOT
ADOPTED

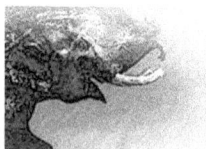

LITANIES
NOT
ADOPTED

A Collection of Poetry

R.B. Warren

Contents

For, of course,

Barbara Laubach Warren

and in memory of

Laura, Robbie, Keane, Yoko, and Sandy

Barbara;

Thank you for all the things
I never said thank you for.
Thank you for your love,
        and for the kids,
        and for the grandkids.

Thank you for being excited
when you see boiled zucchini
on the stove,
for making your time into beauty.

Thank you for trusting me;
for giving me the space
and time to trust myself.

Thank you for remembering
more of me that is good
than is bad.

Thank you for caring
when it was a harder thing to do,
and for speaking the truth
even when I wasn't listening.

Thank you for your patience,
for your waiting.

Thank you for your elegance
and for your grace

in garden boots.

Thank you for the quiet times,
and watching when I got too quiet.
Thank you for your gardens
and your excellence with critters.

Thank you for the place you've given God.
        For the mornings.
        and the evenings.

Thank you for my life with you.

Love,
Bob

The Newcomers Meeting

The first circle forms
around the seekers and the sought,
the young, the old,
the paid for, and the bought.

We settle in, tidy,
the planned and planners.
We are civil, conscious
of our privacy and manners.

Then <u>she</u> came -
   brown coat - brown slacks -
   barely there except for pain.

"Who are we
   and why are we here"
Went quietly around our circle
until it met her fear,
   and her bird fluttering hands,
   and her husband trouble,
   and her need for human touch,
   and her eyes.

The meeting coughed, averted, and resumed.
She had to leave, got up, and left the room.
What remained was her face,
the fact of crucifixion
in this most Christian place,
and the horrible stench
of never touching civil grace.

Ecce Signum

Weather permitting,
the clothes for the poor
are separated

                        on the ground
at Casa Juan Diego.
At this place,

                        pain
and pinto beans,
fear and hunger

                        mock
the ordinary stations
of the cross.

To the east, bishops caress
cathedral walls

                        and within
that hardened coolness
barely wash their softened hands
to whiteness
and barely cleanse
their corporate hearts of blood.
The theft that allowed
the catholic and apostolic
to enter Texas, somehow, by
or through the grace of "whatever,"
still allows the cool of
cathedral walls, and the washing
of the bishops' hands,
and the softness,
and the heartless

disappearance
of Jesus Christ.
                              And so
the Sanhedrin still sits,
and the actors still play emperor,
and the emperors still play God,
and the crucifixions continue.

   The crucifixions continue
when the alien land is daily sanctified
with the blood of the innocent,
   when the widows and children
   are daily pierced by the power
   of law and lawlessness,
when the homeless and hungry
remain homeless and hungry,
   when corporate benevolence
   celebrates its greed,
when the silent, motionless observer
still sits alone at night
with only these words
and his hypocrisy for comfort.

Easter Sunday - 1984

It is proclaimed:

> "Christ is risen!
> Hosanna!
> Blessed is he who comes
> In the name of the Lord!"

For the re-creation of this day,
the Braves play the Astros in Atlanta.
A tennis match is called "Nutra-Sweet"
and is played in Florida,
in a town called Amelia.
And in a television docu-drama,
Le Pape au courant is played
by an actor named Finney,
which, in Italian,
is judgment enough.

It is
a quiet day in Lebanon,
                    in Cyprus.
Children starve quietly
        to death in Chad,
Ghana, and Mozambique.
Death is always quiet
in Huntsville,
in Gulag,
in Johannesburg.
Death is quiet
where shrinks cull
the unacceptable

and call it science,
where prisons are called Rosharon,
where deep
in the caves of inhumanity
adaptable reptiles grow skins
on their eyes
and dream horrible new realities.

Death is quiet
in the blue lit, bored
rooms of America
where the fathers
and the mothers
and the children
sit to re-create this day
absorbed solely
   in the excitement
of the final score.

On this day, at this time,
there are not tears enough
to wash away this filth.

Only blood will do.

Diane Reed

Your question -
How challenged
in the "heart and guts,"
the "bowels"
of the Gospel
am I?

Four hundred, five hundred
year old words here!

Tyndale, Cranmer,
Ridley and Latimer,
death stalkers all,
challenged, believed,
and fed fires
from within the Gospel "guts,"
the "bowels,"
the literal "inner parts"
of the common Greek,
the koinos of the Testament.

Thank God,
not the "affections" of the RSV
or the "yearnings" of the NEB.
Indeed, dear sister,
how challenged
in the guts of the Gospel?
Holding fast,
in a two word answer,

to Jesus Christ.
Clinging to one word,
first and last,
Jesus Christ.

Clinging to Christ with -
and only by -
the grace bestowed,
not earned or owed.

Only given, and then,
the grace once more
to receive is given.
The challenge by grace.
The guts by grace.
The grace by grace
even the death by grace.

Thanksgiving Morning

It was the same this morning -
        the alarm clock going off - the too early
realization of uneasy sleep -
the house chilled overnight -
        the cough - the coffee -
the slight imperfect ablution -
the day old Levi's and the first day shirt -

Then Barb wakes, wonders why, and says
        "Guess I'll go with you today."
In our state,
if we are two disguised J.C.'s,
all creation's in a bind.
Check the readings -
Thessalonians, John,
no saint's special day.

Then more coffee, coat, and car.
Outside, the overcast is low -
the East End lights itself - 4 blocks
to drive and then the church -
grey, solid, and old
in the artificial AM night.

We are the first - hope God
there's more - Then Gordon comes,
and we go through the door
to sit before the cross
and candles still unlit -
and Jeri comes - And then,

thank God again, comes George.
We are here.
We kneel.
And Gordon leads.

Morning Prayer

Praises, sins,
songs, and words
blur together
until the tears
unbidden come
and fall with centuries
of practice
upon the pages of the book.

We give our thanks,
are blessed - amen.
Barb reaches out
her hand - and then
within that singularity
of time and space
His presence comes
to fill the place
and I hear
with unaccustomed grace,
            "If not you,
                    Who?"
            "If not now,
                    When?"

Auschwitz Sunday Morning

An Anniversary of the Liberation of Auschwitz

Is it true that God
gave their killers a choice?
Is it true that God
who knows every leaf
      on every tree
      and every hair
      on every head
said
- finally and completely -
"NONE OF MY BUSINESS!"?
Is it true
that on this morning
of mournings
we gathered
for a regulation
celestial, feel-good hour?
Is it true that God
has anything to say
worth listening to?
I think it's time
to change the channel.

Stewardship Sunday

The appurtenances of control,
the car, the house, health,
the reductio ad absurdum
reduced to parables of power,
of plus and minus,
of black and red,
in subject fear of the bottom line.
Oh, the lilies of the field,
how they count!
And the birds of the air,
how they render unto Caesar!
And oh, how the sojourner drinks
from the wells of the familiar!

Lazarus, et al

Deep in the twisting cave, the helix ravels out.
The spiral smudges, twinned and tethered
so tightly until now, emerge above the table
in a pre-germanic, deeply insane face.
All things are made of it.
The eagle flight and rabbit run.
The corn, corn husk, and pollen dust.
The wool, the shawl, the warp and woof.
The table and the face.
Found, gathered, is the gift of thanks.
Sown, tended, becomes the seed of death.
Sage requires no victim. Pollen does.
Who cooperates -- operates together --
God with us or us with God?
Spirit is the measure of eternity,
is now, is gift, is found, is thank you.
Must do, over time, appeases, pleases,
marks, reduces place to a desire.
Hills, rocks, rams, rituals and liturgies,
co-ordinates of fear, shape the edge of blood.
Anchored in time and place,
the gift in love is taken, given back in pain
and back and back again, circles upon circles,
until the earth itself is soaked in Gift.
You need not need, he says,
            the free and needless one,
                full quit of time and space,
this one last time, this one last place,
here and now is the only gift
you cannot hold and mock me with.

Farmers of the spirit will not see
outside the circle or the line,
or that the sacrifice of blood
is not within the wine.
Grapes gathered, trod upon,
tended to a substitute,
not the thing itself.
The thing itself said, No more.
No more the stench of rendered gift,
of blood, of death.
The thing itself was rendered, and did bleed,
did die. And upon return did say, No more.
The cave, the light just barely there,
the spiral helix warped into
a sacrifice that cannot be.
The thing itself
stands entrance bound,
turns, locks eyes, and says,
Come out with me.

Sunday AM

The place is a quarter full
or most empty now
depending on your point of view
or where you sit
for Sunday AM Eucharist.

There was a time sometime ago
when not a seat could be found
much after ten.
The place was more than full
with household folks,
singles, doubles, untempered ones,
who, not yet burned,
unsullied by circumstance,
could find the time and grace
to hold the seats for those
who later came to be among
the best, the most, of all their lives
here, somehow, made most real
on Sunday AM Houston time.

It was a be good, feel good,
real good time - with songs
and dance - smiles and prayers -
to help make consecrate
the elements of Christ among His people,
back when folks thought they knew what
was what and how to do the will of God,
somehow, made most real
on Sunday AM Houston time.

There was no great sin
that killed the work -
only the sullen fear of solitude
that forgot the singer
for the song.
Now we wondering sit
and gaze upon these moths
of Christ, pinned, cased, and brightly lit
within our chloroform of history and hurt.

Dear Souls

We do not fit a manufactured world
where time, less sacred, is money.
We do not fit because we wait,
and listen and watch,
because we exorcise the time.
We do not fit because we know
that orders are meant to kill Moses,
who ran and paused,
and paused again,
and paused,
until the bush caught fire
and his attention.

In-house Memo

How shall we speak
within this realm
of petty thieves,
whose lies
are their only knowing?
We speak of hell,
and they see
falling stocks.
We speak of Satan,
and they think
old and simple thing
no longer
bumping in the night.
We speak of blessing,
and they think ownership.
We speak of curse,
and they see AIDS.
We speak of love,
and they hear sex.
We speak of truth,
and they are lost.
Perhaps we speak too much.
And yet, God spoke,
and few heard,
and God did,
and few saw.
Perhaps we do enough
to speak and do the truth.

No Kidding

Keeper of the promise,
what promise have you kept?
Your feel good, stand up,
sit down, eight hour day
felt good in the gathered closeness
of your numbers, in the comfort
of your safety,
in the self-same sanity
of your cookie cutter Jesus.
But where are you today
when the kid's still hungry,
and her mother's still beaten?
Where are you, your numbers,
your safety, your shared insanity.
Where – today?
When the only warmth of the overpass
is the body losing heat beneath it?
Where are you today?
Today when your gathering has been
ungathered by your lies, your
cowardice, and your comfort?
Where are you in your prepaid
ten thousands when the one
who paid for you still walks
unknown, unsought, unloved
among you?
Where are you
in the rest of your lives?
Please, in the name of God,
shut your mouths.

Keep contained within you
your mockery of Hosanna.
Keep still the Hallelujah
of your contagion, your fear,
of your Mammon serving lies.
In time, perhaps, your eyes will open.
Perhaps, your ears might hear.
Perhaps, in grace, your minds might
crack, perhaps your hearts might open.
Perhaps and perhaps.
But until that time, that grace,
in the name of God,
Keep still the tongues
that mock the praise of God.

Litanies Not Adopted

I.

Easter in Socorro, at the sunrise service
of many denominations, and what is being said?
What devilment is being played?
What soft spoken-ness is passing over
the first of the first born risen dead?
"It's so nice to see you again."
"The holidays bring everybody out, heh?"
"Good weather. The wind's not bad."
"Well, lookee here, who's here."
"Naw, Mom's not doin' too good."
"He's that new Presbyterian fellow."
"Nice man."
"The best we do is what we do."
"Do you have a program?"
"And you", the accuser asks,
"can you ask more?"
There is no need to ask
to be accused of judgement.

II.

The processional we mocked this morning
began before the beginning.
But for today, it started from bedrooms,
and showers and cars and, once again,
from Antonia's porch.
We are farther now from the day of blood,

than those back then, who saw the fire
and the smoke and read the words in stone.
This new revelation smelled,
not of fire, but of sweat,
was immediate and proximate.
It talked and walked, and ate with us.
And taught and loved. And everything
was clearer and more clouded
in the everyday-ness of it.
Carved in flesh and bone,
and wind and hair,
and hunger and surfeit,
and laughter and tears,
it was perhaps too close to us.
Too much of us was in it.
Birthed and raised among us,
it was more like us than we like it.
This new image of the image,
this mirror of our likeness,
turned creation on its head.
It was not position, but possibility,
not distance, but nearness,
not judgement, but laughter,
that brought out the hate.
God now wholly included
our taste and our hunger,
our tears and our love,
our soaring and crawling,
our stardust, our hate.

III.

The books and bricks are both too frail,
and the universe too small,
to do much more than point the way.
No place there is for such a thing
except within us. And He knew it.
The ones who hated
somehow knew it too.
In the calculus of hate,
first find the blood, then the murder.
Find the murder, then the lie.
Find the lie, and then the idol.
Find the idol, then the fear.
And the fear once more
will lead to blood.
The confusion of the relative,
the derived, the tertiary,
lies enfolded in the desire of fear,
and such desire always kills,
and such desired way back when
in torture and murder,
that flesh be crushed,
that blood must flow,
that the man must die.
That the Sabbath may come.

IV.

Did they, the ones who ran
away and those who stayed,
remember the last instructions?
Did they, in remembrance,
re-member? In the night,
after the old and before
the new, did they dare
take up the bread and cup
of Saturday despair?

                    And what of her?
                    Did she ever look back
                    to Cana?
                            Or to Elizabeth?
                    Did she ever wonder
                    what if her yes
                    had been a no?
                    Did she remember
                    Gabriel waiting,
                    Heaven hushed,
                    and a world
                    hanging on her words?

And of Him --
In the realm of death,
on the crying ground
of Gethsemane,
in the blood soaked memory
of the dirt,

did He finally and completely
come to know
our terror of creation?

V.

This morning, Dear Heart, the statement
of blood was approximated
by clueless mediators,
as if they knew the wind
and hunger of God.
From the start, obviously
and in good order, it was clear
this was no Francis, speaking truth.
          (The birds, unloved, would not shut-up.)
A word (whatever it was) was spoken,
invoked and called upon. The cup
was blessed. The wafers broken.
to the comfortable and bored,
some hope was given,
some sustenance restored.
The caped crusader gave out bread,
and Mrs. Robert (Bertie) Williams poured.

VI.

"And you, in your arrogance, pointing
(You always point) at what we cannot see."

But would you if you could?

VII.

The cost is not too much.
Or even much.

The cost is being born
within some form of freedom
and of being, of growing
into some other form,
some dimensioned fleshing out,

from before dimensions,
length and breadth,
within that visibility of love
we call the Christ, the Breath.

There is nowhere in that.

No here. No there.
Only this place
where time meets eternity
and love becomes grace.

It is exactly right, exactly now,
to do this thing
that we were born to do.

VIII.

And as for the rest of it,
we do the best we can,
sometimes,
and as for your question,
of course you're loved.
Of course.

Three for Me

Heavenly Father,
am I to misunderstand again?
Shall I
        in some strange shape of love
provide the cause of hunger?
Or the proper use of usury?
Will the sweet salt tears of Sunday
serve only to garnish my hypocrisy?

        Holy of Holies,
        The Most High,
        how do I approach you?
        In those eternities of your touch,
                in the lifting presence of your love,

        I disappear
        and am complete.

Abba -
    At times
to even thank you
presumes too much.
    At times,
within the midday
take-a-meeting
memo madness,
I waken
    to my own rock,
    my own Bethel,
without a verily or truly

to my name.
    with only,
           "Wow. He was here!
              and I didn't even know it!"

A Sequence: By What Authority?

Magically jumping

From the Sunday
of Palms to Easter,
the elder said,
      "Your work lacks victory."
The other paused and said,
come close.
Have some courage.
See these hands and feet,
this touch, these tracks.
See the prints of history.
Come close and look
into these eyes that mirror
more than surety.
Search this soul
for signs of vacancy.
See these dreams,
and hear these prayers,
each more solid
even than your heart.
Come close
and listen to this blood.
Taste this laughter.
Savor this love.
See His breath
breathed on and in
this dirt framed
love of God.
Come and see.

Have courage.
Come close.

Grandma

Two murdered daughters'
daughters, ages 6 and 8,
the butchered spinal tap
a quarter century ago,
the question in the eyes
of making it a few more,
twelve she smiles,
years for the younger
one to reach eighteen.
No food, she says, and another
thirty minutes to the next pill
that kills the pain and marks her life
in segments so finite and perfect
that even Jesus weeps.

Mel

Twenty explosions – fusions,
fissions in the Pacific –
with whatever group
he doesn't, can't,
won't say, have left
for him a friendless life,
Without family, facing

the approaching blackness
of his death
in a twelve foot trailer
with neither food nor heat,
transparent to the bombs
he watched, the radiation
he absorbed, and the love
he cannot find.

Woman

Grey haired, glasses,
slightly square in shape,
fifty five, alone,
no friends or family.
No one except her dog.
No thing except her master's degree.
Shattered, she sleeps
with both of them
each night
    in her car
on these streets of terror
that no man will ever know.

Covered by the Blood

A shrink calls, a regular call,
a nice guy.
A client needs some food.
And then the weirdness comes.

"All people need pride," he says.
One of the seven deadlies, I think,
but say, "Dignity perhaps is better."
"Pride is important," he says,
"A sense of accomplishment, of helping,
of doing something important."
Yeah, I think, like getting a job
and feeding your family - but silence
is golden I think and keep it.
"A friend of a friend," he says,
"Works in a hospital,
and the friend tells me
they need blood."
Well usually, I say,
they do a media blitz,
and everybody knows about it.
"I was thinking," he says, "about the poor
and the sense of pride
they could have."
I say, Hold it!
Are you really going where
I think you're going?
You want hungry folks
to give blood?
(No chance for silence to blossom.)
You want people who can't
even get admitted to hospitals,
who don't have the money,
the insurance,
to give their blood
(By now I'm shouting.)
to people who don't
give a crap about them?

Why the hell don't you ask
your rich buddies to give their blood?
(I'm out of control now – screaming at him.)
Jesus, Jesus, man
Don't you get it?
Even a little?
The rich are rich because
they've already bled the poor.
Understand?
No more blood to give.
"This needs more thought,"
he says.
Yeah right. Take care.

No Name

Gang raped two nights ago,
she cannot speak. But with
the words, "You are among friends."
we both shudder, and with, "No one
will hurt you here,"
we both begin to cry.
She is curled in upon herself,
sitting, not fetal, but hunched
upon the pain.
And I sit, invisible with her,
an old, grey bearded, useless man
who can no longer fix the pain
and make it go away.

The Place of Evil

Early images aside,
there is no book lined study
in this life.
No verdant walks, no walking sticks.
No Lake Country.
No sherry, port, or wedded couplets.
No climbing of Ben Nevis.
The study here is of fear lined faces,
of eyes in pain.
The walk is through the stubble
of ruined lives and violence.
The aperitif is tears of rage
at one more lost and ravaged kid.
The climb is to the hill of skulls,
laid waste and bare with more,
far more this time,
than apathy and hate.

A Correspondence

Dearest Heart of All;

No wager of a single Job
is worthy of these times.
Wager, Dear Heart, an entire world
of pain and death.
Wager the structural re-alignment
of these babies torn limb from limb
and made to fit
a spreadsheet bottom line
of delimited precision
and surgical cleanliness.
Wager the tears of mothers
holding the bodies of these babies
ripped and torn from life.
Wager the lives of men
who have no thoughts
of righteousness or holiness,
who think only of the hunger
and thirst of their little ones.
Wager the response of those
who never saw the lily of the field
or the pearl buried next to it.
Wager the ease and comfort
of the writer of these words.
Wager, if you will,
the collateral damage

of your ministry.
And tell us, please, up front,
just once, just who is betting,
Who's the pot,
and who the hell is dealing.

Letter #3

Dearest Heart of All;

Thank you for all of it.
You know I have no
other place to go.
No other place where
there is such love.
No place below.
No place above.
Only here where broken
is prelude to whole.
Only here is spoken
the forgiveness
of my pratfalls and platitudes,
my anger and my attitudes.
I knew before the first note
there never was a bet,
least of all a game.
And yet I chose to see the blood
and so forgot your name.
Forgive me, Lord, my red ball nose,
my baggy pants, my size thirty shoes.
Forgive the grease paint
and the twisting of the news.
In the midst of ordinary lives,
I ask forgiveness
for all my faults and all my lies.

And plead your mercy
upon my clownish hows
and all my clownish whys.

Letter #5

Dearest Heart of All;

Thank you.

Thank You.
Yes.
Maranatha.

Sequel-9-One-One

It is best for you,
no matter the consequence,
to have no memory.
       Let the grief be grief
       without history.
Let there be no time
before the horror.
       Divorce the moment
       from the context.
Shrink the world
to your skin.
Circle the wagons.
Incorporate yourself,
and stay the center
of your universe.

You will waken one day
from this nightmare,
and when you waken,
you will know
that nothing has changed,
that your leaders and priests
are men and women of honor,
that your country
is intact and moral,
that you are safe, fully safe.
and further, on that day,
no child will die
for your bananas,
no women

will be raped and killed
for your tennis shoes,
no man
will be murdered
for your distraction.
You will waken that day
in the sure knowledge
that the poor play no part
in the privilege and comfort
of your life,
that you are innocent,
and that somehow,
in the activity of your god,
the game has begun again.

The Boonies

Dear Heart,

There is plenty of work
here in the outskirts
feeding the others' hunger,
dressing up folks who can't
afford to buy their own,
holding the hands
through the dark night.

Letting some know
if they're good enough for you
they're good enough for me.

The work is here.
Busy enough.
Real enough.
Even sometimes quiet enough.
Maybe that's it.
Just quiet enough.
Just for awhile.

Quiet and still,
here in the boonies,
away from the temple,
and the surety of the priests,
and the blood the crowd
called for when they saw
you really meant it.

Another Day in the Kingdom

It is clear.
The hungry cry for righteousness,
and no one answers.
No one speaks for the orphan.
The fatherless perish in the silence
of the widows' eyes.
Food is scarce save for the satisfied and the full.
And only the rich now speak for the land.
Why should not this place
be called a desolation?
Why should not
destruction and famine
overtake this horror?
Why should not
a witness host
come forth to testify?

Even the steam grates of your center
bear witness against you.
Even dumb metal,
even rising vapors,
speak of your sin.
Your leaders - your choices -
your shamans - your priests
all fall full scale
from the excrescence
of your hatefulness.
Your dogs you treat
with more concern
than your brothers.

It is no wonder that
even your language is broken,
and the words of your mouth
serve only to confuse your lies.
You have passed your children
through the fire of your hate,
and now your beds are made
uneasy by the blood thirst
of the small ones among you.
You have worshipped your own vileness.
Climbed a tree to lie when truth was at your feet.
Sold what was not for sale.
Bought what cannot be paid for.
The pain of others
has become your sustenance.
Your tables are set
and your bellies are filled
with the pain and suffering of the poor.
With the blood and bone of the orphan
you plan your tomorrow.
As if tomorrow still belonged to you.
As if the dawn of a new day
will not surround your recompense.
As if God will not
in justice
repay your mockery.

Carlos

Carlos was
     the Ragman
who slept
behind the pharmacy
on Central Avenue
in the alley
even in the wintertime
until somebody
snuffed him
with a match
and gasoline
and smoked
his cardboard
boxes and left
a large black stain
on the back alley
wall of the
Central Avenue Pharmacy
in Albuquerque
New Mexico
One night
during the second
Week of January
in the year
of our Lord Jesus Christ
nineteen hundred
and eighty-eight.
His death became news
when two hundred
nameless ones met

to share the memory
of his street filled life
and somehow celebrate
the whole burnt offering
of Carlos
        the Ragman
a holocaust of one.

On The Street

There were four of them,
urban types, not res,
drunk as skunks,
waiting to get in
at nine o'clock in the morning.
They carried a note
from a black robe
who knew next to nothing
about them or their lives.
My Brothers Of The Street
he called them.
Please help he wrote.
He lied. Get them away
from me is what he meant.
Four - too drunk to let in.
One was chosen, most upright,
to shop for free, for all.
Shoes, shirts, some time inside,
a coffee and a donut and some talk.
This one alone was from Isleta,
wife and two kids there,
and him in drunken exile.
The Isleta judge who judged him
has a son, he says, who sells dope
but no, he says, he kicks me off
for being drunk. The bastard.

Next Sunday, 8:20AM,
the black robe, now white,
looks up, with bread

in his hands and sees
the four, drunk as skunks,
weaving up to him
communion bound.
Bread my ass he thinks they say.
Get the wine.
This time there is no time
to write a note, to plead for help.
These crazy Indians,
Oh God forgive,
drunken indigenous ones,
have become his
Brothers Of The Inappropriate.
He offers bread. Forbids the wine.
The first scout engages him directly.
The second sweeps the flank
and staggers, arms outstretched,
toward the cup of Mogen David
hot damn Kosher Concord Wine.
No one maybe since Saint Francis
had sought the blood with greater need.
The need was unfulfilled.
As always with the whites
it was the numbers, always numbers,
that prevailed. Mouse scurrying
Deacons, ushers imprecating
muttered curses, exiled
within themselves
the reservation of propriety.
If words could kill (they do),
the four would have died that day
between the sanctuary and the altar,
killed as the old time prophets were,

trying to get drunk on God.

As it was, his god spoke through
the robed and temple vested one.
It said, in full reverberation,
you are always welcome here.
But not like this. Please leave.
And so they did.

The bloodied, pierced,
and tortured one
was there that day,
And when the ushers
ushered out the door
the four defeated ones,
the one whose tears
are sometimes cold
and hard as diamonds
wept warm and wet,
got up and left.
And joined his family
on the street.

The Bish and Me

Oh God, more stories
of war.
       We meet
with two thousand years
between us.
Resting on one,
the horses, tanks, and regiments,
the distant carnage.
The other,
the night fighter,
hidden in plain sight,
the silent, awful,
closeness of the blade.
We talk as if it matters
to explain the blessing
of the scars.
A kind of peace is offered.
Come in he says.
The nights are colder now.
Your bones are older now.
Come in and rest.
There still is time.
Come in to what
The other says.
Your roof is gone,
Your windows are broken,
and more than your doors
are unhinged.
More pronouncements,
postures. As if our courtesy

could bridge the gap.
Yet within this civility
of manners,
each knows the other knows
it is the one
upon whose heart we dance
who bleeds.

Detroit and, and, and, and, and,,,,,,and, no buts,,,,,,,

Detroit was a really great city in the early sixties,
before the drugs and guns came in big-time
and the cops spread their paranoia all over the place
and the people began to pick up on it
and go just as crazy as the cops were,
and cabs would actually pick you up and take you anywhere
without that bullshit bulletproof glass between the backseat
and the driver like the liquor stores
had between the customers
and the booze and those spinarama
deals for passing the money
in and the bottles out,
and you could go anyplace in the city
without being hassled or mugged or shot at.

Anyway I had this date, third time is the charm right?
This one was gonna be all out –
The Wine Cellars and then the Drome
and then the Unstabled and then if everything goes good
my apartment for the first time.

So I pick her up and we go to the Cellars,
and she's never had French cooking before,
or even wine with a cork in the bottle,
or a place where the menu is in French.
And the wine guy comes out and the rest of the guys
know me and I order for both of us and she says after,
it's great, and I'm some kind of man of the world,
and how it's all really cool.

After that we head to the Drome,
which was a bowling alley called the Hippodrome
out on Dexter Avenue with a lounge attached to it
where all the great jazz players would play in Detroit,
and Horace Silver was playing that night,
and like almost always I was the only honkie
in the place, and the waitresses knew me there too,
and her eyes got big when we got a table
right next to the stage
and, Jesus Christ, in the low light and the cigarette haze,
and the Cutty, and how she was dressed and how she sat,
and how she was just so goddamned beautiful,
and she wasn't even trying.

We left in the middle of the last set and got a cab
and stopped at a liquor store to buy two pints of vodka
cause the Unstabled sold only coffee no booze
and charged fifty cents a cup so what you'd do
is get a coffee and drink half of it, and then fill it to the top
with vodka, and nurse it for the next hour
while all the great players were coming in from the Drome,
the Continental and Baker's Keyboard,
and they'd play together for the next four five hours
and it was winter and when we walked out
around seven thirty in the morning, a couple
maybe three inches of snow had fallen,
and she was wearing high heels and couldn't walk
in the snow without freezing her feet and just then
            – What a night –
a cab comes by and we get to my apartment
after being up for twenty four hours,
and eating and drinking,

With the great music and talking
and somehow not even getting high
and we got undressed, and into and around each other,
and slowly and quietly really, I mean really,
made some love with each other. When I woke up,
she was in the kitchen cooking bacon
bare ass except for an old darkroom apron of mine
and she looked at me and shut the burners off,
and we went back to bed and did the wild thing,
and then I lifted the shades and the light came in the room
and I saw the marks low down on her stomach
just above her hair, and I said, What the fuck are they?
and I knew what the fuck they were,
and she said, No big deal just skin poppin',
and I said, Oh, Jesus H. Fucking Christ,
how I hate that fucking shit. I fucking hate that shit.
Get goddamn dressed and I'll get you a cab.

She got a cab.
I got cold bacon……..
And the clap.

This Time

There is so little time
To say these thats –
- that I have loved
   the taste and smell
   of Rigel, Arcturus,
   and Betelgeuse –
      - that constellations
   are beyond my pale
   of ardor –
- that there is no better
  time than looking upon
  the face of love,
  (she blushes still) –
- that the hole
  in my shirt
  is of surpassing
  strangeness –
- that when I call to God
  and hear the stillness
  that at the least
  the silence has been broken
  by the sound of God –
- that we all
  have been called
  by name not to answer
  but by invitation to speak –
- that Bach wrote
  what God would sing –
- that I aspire,
  conspire, aspirate,

and consecrate
by that presence
chosen, full well,
within me,
to both big bang
and small whimper –
- that most of all
  it has been granted
  that we love –
- and that that,
  that wonder we face,
  is the most lovely of all –
- only that we love.

Note From the Field -- 12-24

Dear Blessed Heart;

Tomorrow you are scheduled to come
again to where you have always been.
Still so few to guard you,
to breathe over your newness
and hope beyond this night.
    (Forgive the tone, but
     The eve is always like this.
     The day before always dead tired.)
Some questions:
Will the heavenly host announce you,
or is it up to us?
Are the gifts to be the same,
or will this paper do?
Herod knows you're here,
but will Joseph listen again?
Will he take you to Egypt again?
Will he keep you safe for another day,
another Herod?
The soldiers need not come again.
They have never left.
The babies have not stopped dying.
Rachel has never stopped weeping.
The bloody blades were put away long ago.
Pens, pencils, and counted beans
now do the work of death.
For the last month or so,
You've been for sale.
Judging by the market,

the only problem with Judas
was his timing. Today, it was
pork bellies, heating oil, and you.
Given all of this, you still
will come, won't you? The little ones
still need you, and they will know you.
The drunks, the whores, and I
still need you. We need your arm,
your eyes, your breath, your laughter.
This place in all the blood and death and gore
still needs you.
You will come, Dear One, won't you,
and be among us? And once more
love us into being?

New Life

The two – the couple –
the big and barrel chested –
seem, when seen together,
to be toppling toward
some future, terrifying sidewalk.

They were once –
when he was a fitter
at South Texas Nuke,
and making the long green,
before the shits hit Houston,
and Brown and Root
laid off all but the most
tried and true thieves
and ass kissers --
quite acceptable
in the Sunday kind of churches
that are the second
worst thing
about Pasadena, Texas.

They – the couple –
and his – now her – son
somehow fit in Pasadena
on every Sunday morning
before the job paid out
and the money stopped
and the beer
had to be drunk less often
and more intensely.

They fit – they said –
but only on the edge,
and when they drifted off,
the center of the puzzle
never felt the tug.
No one ever called,
or if they did, called back.
When they finished
passing through the place
and left for here,
it was
            - just us three
                    - off to the real west
                    - off to the clean air
                    - off to the somewhere else
            - to the new start
            - to the new beginning
            - to the new life.
They believed the lie
for one night
on the road
until the first drunk
when he hit her
on the shoulder
of Interstate 40
just outside Tucumcari.
He thought the kid
was asleep in the back seat.

Now, at night, settled here
in three rooms of home,
after six or eight
or ten beers,

he slams her
against the wall,
and the next door whatever
turns up the volume
on his favorite
Black Sabbath album.
She says he falls asleep
afterwards
and cries.
Remembering perhaps
the unaccepted shame
or maybe, the beaten,
big breasted wife –
who brings in the money
by tending bar
and shaking whatever
she can
four nights a week
at the Amvets Hall.

The child is without friends,
and would not be a friend
to one who would be his.
There is a feral watchfulness
about him –
a wordy silence.
His fear is not of them,
but of himself.
He has seen
in thirteen years
far more than enough.
And one day,
it will be wondered

how this small young man,
obviously so well spoken,
and so polite,
could possibly have done
what he did.

Jeri Lee Hooks

Why?
Why did you not answer the knock
on the door?
Ten, twenty, thirty times
we knocked and called your name,
but you did not answer.
We called and you did not come.

There are too many questions now.
Was Christ not clear among us?
Did you need more love
than we could give?
Was the pain in our own eyes
too clear to you?
Did the blindness of our love
frighten you?
Was it too much or not enough?
There are too many questions now.

He had a name for you.
He called you from before your birth
his beloved.
He gifted you to us,
and you now have returned
the gift before its time,
and come unbidden into the peace of God.

We called for you and you did not come.
He played for you and you did not dance.

Was there nowhere even a whisper,
an echo, a reflection of His love?

If you were here,
I would ask your forgiveness,
for what I do not know. Perhaps
to start again our conversation.
But our talk has been broken
before its time.
The timely speech
must now await eternity,
where the conversations
ended in tears begin again,
in the holy, holy, holy
praise of His name.

Goin' Round

The bloody
bloodthirsty constructions,
the ones you coerced and pimped
and turned from sweetness and light,
the ones you trained to kill,
trained to maim,
trained for fun to fill
the gutters with rivers
of baby's blood,
these ones you trained and sent away
to cut for you the cost
of your bananas,
your shirtsleeves, your oil,
and your comfort
will soon
have no place to go
but home,
and they are bringing
with them
their terrible
and terrifying
one-eyed children.
Their terrible
and terrifying
and thirsty
one-eyed children.

In Memoriam – Eddie O'Brien

Eighty years ago,
when Eddie O'Brien was born,
his too drunk father didn't
make it to the hospital.
Eddie turned out to be
a strange kind of kid.
  Epilepsy – little seizures,
eyes open, staring off into space
for a minute or two or three,
and then the big ones rolling on the floor
and people jumping on him
so he wouldn't hurt himself.
They found some kind of medicine that kept
the seizures mild most of the time,
and Eddie grew up almost normal.
He got a pretty good job,
and met a girl – beautiful, really beautiful.
She liked him. He liked her.
Two epileptics in love. They got married.
Got an apartment. Had a baby. And were happy.
One night she had a grand mal,
or something in bed,
choked on her vomit,
rolled on the baby and died.
The baby died too. Suffocated.
Eddie woke up to a dead wife and a dead baby.
Got them buried somehow and stopped
taking his meds. Had a big seizure
one morning cooking breakfast
and fell on the stove. Fried his face.

And went down real fast from there.
The last time any of us saw Eddie
was when two cops were beating him
with nightsticks in an alley off of Grand River.
My brother yelled at the cops,
and tried to stop them, saying Eddie wasn't drunk,
he just had epilepsy. But they turned
and started beating on my brother.
When they finished with him,
they threw Eddie in the back of the cop car.
We called precinct stations and hospitals
and the morgue for days and days, and weeks,
but nobody said they had an Eddie O'Brien.
Eddie lived and died, I suppose, drowned
in tragedy. Nobody probably held him
when or where he died. Or held much
of his memory after he died. Except maybe God.
Or me maybe sometimes.
And now maybe you. Maybe you.
Maybe you becoming two,
or two becoming three,
and when two or three are gathered,
one could hope, two could watch,
for some bubble of singularity,
some cell of information,
some eventful horizon of expectation,
where Eddie smiles beautifully
at his beautiful wife and child,
where nightsticks have become
chrysanthemums and daffodils,
where the violent and vicious ones,
the merchants, the buyers and sellers of souls,
spend endless time and effort

unloading, unsheathing, undoing
their weapons, their mouths and their hands,
of hatred and destruction,
of wiping clean their spotless spreadsheets
of horror, and unshriven,
blaming the blood for the blade.
One can hope there is abroad some dysphasia of purpose,
some disquietude within the cells that seeks
the unlicensed learning of a new language,
an almost unheard, almost unknowable,
barely there, "Hello, I love you."

One can hope.

The Numbers Prophet and the Boys

1.

Clearly, distinctly,
    At whatever kilocycles
    Of Windsor-Dee-troit radio waves, he
    Sunday Broadcast Service said,
    "And now we shall turn
    To the Gospel of Matthew.
    Matthew 5:17."
And he did – and they did –
And it did –the number 517 -
    Fall the next day
At 500 to 1.
And a few small time runners
Tried a get-together
With the woodwork
'Cause they didn't lay it off.
And the selections continued.
    Scripture bein' read on Sunday,
And the numbers falling square
On Monday.
    (Cock bull preachers been in short supply
        And in the novelty, he was believed.)
Three more weeks – scripture called out Sunday,
And numbers comin' through on Monday,
And a whole buncha people
Lettin' they feet take care of business.
    And him –
        A rising shot
        Ghetto cosmic balance

In a beautiful brocade of beads
And process
          Did grow
And prosper with the Times
And the News
          And the Free Press
Turnin' a prelim
Into a main event,
And him thinking a set-up
Was B.Y.O.B.

2.

Burrhead pretty young preacher boy
With think chinks of darkness voodoo
And Roman magic slanted into Jesus,
Comin' into Birmingham too slick, slim, and jellied.
Black carbon in the rough
With a mind making diamonds,
He came, not David, but a patient
Rag wearing Absalom fearing
No trees and no Jehovah.

And he believed in him
          And they believed in him,
Which was enough, enough
For all but the old ladies,
          The quick old ladies,
Who could not see within
          The inner circle of his sanctum
Their smiling, hairless sons.

Hue was nothing.
It was clit that cursed.
Salvation became one in the same.
It was mothers and sons,
        Or nothing at all.
Birmingham became
No thing at all.

3.

Still young maybe,
        When they run him,
Him and his Mama
Out of Birmingham,
        (Talk about scared straight hair
            Somebody laughed,
            But mostly old women
            Cried at being older now.)
On a railway ticket, at night,
        Him and his Mama,
        And him still young
Maybe.

4.

        Hunger
Brought him to Detroit.
Up through down,
In the assembled quickness
Of the Valley,

The Bottom would be reached.
Up through down,
The Big D,
      Detroit,
      Destroyer of minds,
      Breaker of bodies,
Called out the answer to his hunger.

5.

The Prophet learned
The advantage
      All Whiteys need
Need only be an honest one.
In grace, and a need
For young boys, he grew safe
In his vulnerability,
And grew large
In his vulnerability,
And worshipped
      Young boys
At the coming of the age.
And the prophet in being
Became number
And gloried in the oneness
Of the number one –
      Turned within,
Became one with
One – came with one –
The cell upon itself
And cell within cell upon cell

Bore the fruit of the one seed,
Bore the fruit of the one.
"Be fruitful
        And multiply."
"Later for the second half."
Replied the Prophet.

6.

It was need
        Brought him back
        From the Jacktown
        Prison paradise.
It was need
        Saw him rise again.
It was need
        Made the old ladies
        Return once more
        With their sons.
It was need,
        Whitey's need,
        For the fair skinned houseboy
        To keep at least (maybe more)
        Some small segment quiet.
It was Whitey's need
        (So no danger.)
        Brought him back
Full fleshed, flushed, and weary
From his prison exile.

7.

His use was in the duty,
And was duty to spread
Contagion,
       And so was free
Finally to enslave
Within the circle
Of his sickness those
       Who would be free.

8.

Old women check
       For the warmth
Of a son (no matter how cold)
To hold and feel the contractions
Of the minding suck –
       High rumped and small,
They come or listen to feel
No pain.

Weekday women who would be
       Had
By northwestern
Ladies are here and now
Not to be
       Had
On their knees cleaning,
       Scrubbing or cooking
       Or smelling

The porcelain bowls of Whitey's dream,
        To take no
Thing – no rugs no sheets
            No dresses cast
            Off, no food for
            The night
                Of the soul's hunger.
These old women leave
With just themselves (and whole).
A place to be no hurt they find,
And find enough
There within to carry on.
Troubled hearts that only sing
Will never fight,
But think their voices tremor
Will shake with earthquakes might
The prison walls of freedom's night.
            And so he raised the voices,
                In tune, in time,
            And placed upon the enslaved hearts
            The fire making lime
            Of Christian hopes and stillborn starts.

9.

Where was the lamb's bladder,
This condom of the spirit,
When the streets ran red
With black men's blood?

        "It's best to play possum."

And neither Pharisee nor Scribe,
He kicked his lotus blossom
As it stroked his pale brown hide.

His worship rose those days
        With an uncrossed cross,
        Recounted Whitey's ways
        And said, "Yes, sir, you the Boss."

And black men died, were cut and shot
And he, seeing brothers burning in the night,
Said, "Mr. Charley sure is hot!
        Praise Jesus, this ain't our fight."

He remained the riot of Whitey through
Curled tight within the bower of his screw.
        His doves and lick boots flutter and creep
        Around his scented, sainted staff
        Like furied flies and snakes about a garbage heap.

10.

Over time, and in a new time.
He became no longer useful. He faded
Into embarrassment.
In time, brain vessels lost
Or found connection
With the real and broke.
Wrapped in plain white
King Cotton hospital blues,
His neurons stroked apart

And regrouped
Into the silence
Of a wasted terminus
Of tubes and jars.
His body made
The pronouncements
Of input and output,
Of saline-glucose tolerance.
His veins became receptacles
Of unreal energy.
Plastic, throwaway jugs
Put the lie to his life.
His body paralyzed left only
His quiet and finally knowing eyes.

Years before he died – he became
   One more silent, silenced prophet,
One more bare-ass cotton gown,
Bejeweled with piss and vomit,
One more run over, long dead piece
Of America loves me this I know
Road kill shit.

Remember Steve Neale?

His mania early on
was of a soft and
rambling kind.
Whom the Muse does not kill
she makes mad
or, like Homer, blind.

His mother said that,
shortly before his death,
he had,
"Gone off his medicine."

Oh, how lithium
soothes the transition
from madness.
Its single valence
       calms the seas
and creates
       quiet
backwater
       tidepools
           where the sun
with solitary purpose
bleaches white
the neurons of the night.

Ship Channel

Regius
        (A name favored by God
        and disproved by Descartes)
Sullivan
was fired today
at Mobay
Chemical for sucking
in a silo
full of polycarbonate.
His was not the blame --
he covered for a friend.
Job caused cancer
took half a larynx
years ago,
    and in the rasping after voice,
eyes wide with elemental wonder,
all his mind could think to say
    was,
        "I just lost my job."
        "I just lost my job."
        "I just lost my fuckin' job."

A Painter

The names mostly now
with only God
to remember them.
They come at night,
barely haze,
rolling quietly
over the ground of years.
         "What was his name?"
It's their doings
remain clear and clean
now as then.
Everrett. A painter.
On a job
when I was still
green as grass.
Nursed his wife through
her cancer and her death.
And started quietly telling
folks like me that
life wasn't worth living.
There was nothing left
to love, I guess.
Or maybe just to do.
He liked to fish,
had his own pigment box
and a brush that was
never used for paint,
only dusting after a touch up.
He eased one day
in my twentieth year

through a window
five stories up on his lunch hour.
I was working two floors
above him and didn't notice
until the half circle
of amazement gathered
in the alley where he landed.
The kid I was
looked out the seventh
story window and saw
the lump of clothes
and the blood flowing
to the alley drain.
The window he took
his leaving from
was a tight squeeze,
about shoulder high,
it was a climb.
on the ledge, he'd left
with terminal neatness
his glasses
and his dusting brush.
The kid I was
got chose to wash down
the last mess -
blood, teeth, and brains -
that Everrett, the painter,
ever made.
The stupid kid I still
sometimes am
finished washing Everrett
to the sewer,
went back to the shop,

and looked with
new contempt
on the older guys
who'd just got plastered
with their own mortality.
Drank half a glass
of Old Crow
the foreman gave me.
Went home.
Paid for the rest of the day.

Deer Dancer

The toothless one
upstairs in 33
used to be
the mechanic here.
His life is sectioned
like a grapefruit.
Within that packrat
zone of quiet
there is a man
of no small resource
who watched
and tended
for two years
a friend
dying of leukemia,
and then planted a tree
in unsuitable soil
and named the tree Big Bill
to the honor
of his friend.
Today, he said
  "It's easier to grow
   a tree
   than watch
   a friend die."

The Sun

The sun is over the mountain,
and the warm early morning light
points to the table where lately
what work I do is done.
 Write something, it says, anything.
 Mark the page, disturb
 the whiteness of the sheet.
Bring meaning to this less than chaos.
Do something with years and space.
This time, make use. Make do.
Be used.

Barb

The house is almost ready to go,
and I'm sitting
in the dining room
watching us paint.
Remember?
So much love! So much in love!
You've got your blue jeans on,
and that white sleeveless blouse
with the small zipper on the back,
and your loafers,
and there is conversation
warming the winter room.
The paint goes hardest
in the corners
up high,
       and you,
       wiping your forehead
with the back of your hand,
then the tip of your nose,
       almost schoolgirl,
touch up just so
and so and so,
so serious and so in love.
The room is full of us!
Newspapers for drop cloths,
paint spatters for emphasis.
There is love that has lasted
and made everything more
than it ever could have been alone.
Your memory fills my life.

And your fullness empties me.
With heart and soul, I love you.
And I cannot stop hurting.

Bare walls now make me cry.

One

In her mysticism,
she gave up all stimulants and depressants -
cigarettes, alcohol, coffee, and tea.
And alternately depressing and stimulating,
she finally gave up me.

On The Bus

Green dress girl -

- Brown eyes
  in the morning sun -

- My smile is only gladness
  at your beauty.

    <u>or</u>

       brown eyed
           green dress girl
           so golden in the morning sun
           know only that my smile
              is gladness
      & means no harm to you.

       <u>or</u>

       Come off it,
             girl,
         You ain't <u>that</u> fine.

Long Time

Woman -
        I would celebrate your blackness.
But not
        by the ancient tales of murder by the sea,
And not
        by siren songs we never were and could not be.
Neither
        by songs of peaches and cream
And not again
        by tales of journey and dream.
I would leave the dust of the past
on the shoes of the dead,
and celebrate the African Queen -
full moon risen life blood red.

Atoms to eons into sun,
time nexus met with fire,
ages past and yet begun,
universal pyre.
        But all - now all - all now -
this moment would be sung.

It would be heard in the curve of your neck.
And in the woolly closeness of your hair,
would whisper from your shaded triangle
the mystery of Woman everywhere.

To begin.

On Meeting the Ministerial Alliance

The gang of eleven ordained types,
Comes together as some duty calls.
They'd hurt a friend, tried to ruin him,
Scrunged his name, his work, his life.
Baiters and haters all,
Murmurers and gossips,
Bible thumping, heaven humping,
Pseudo-celestial slime balls,
They sit without portfolio,
Chilled within the quiet
Of their windless certitude.
Called upon to repent
Of their affront to God,
And set the weights aright,
They sit circled up,
Coiled upon themselves,
Hoods opened, cowls
And colors revealed,
Rubbing each other down and up,
And up and down.
Whispering,
Whisssssspuuur, they say.
Swaying, closely curled,
Entwined together,
Hydra headed,
Fangs folded toward the rear,
Feigning disinterest,
Slowly ducking and dodging,
Searching for heat,
For life, for life again, to kill.

They yawn most lazily
And flick their tongues,
Tasting the air in welcome

Of me, their enemy.
Praissse Jeesssusss,
They, the choir, in unison hiss,
Anotheeer mee-al.

Abstract:
Double-ought buck is way too much.
410 birdshot's plenty.

On First Meeting the Mission Team

After introductions,
and halfway through the coffee,
the sharp nosed one
who appears to lead says,
"It's the ones with demons
On their shoulders
You have to watch for."
(Oh, boy.)
This one is the pulpit expositor
to three thousand, pew sitting
Sunday types a week.
He explains further that
he studies Sun Tzu, On War,
in order to fight the demons
on the shoulders
of God knows who
in the name of Jesus Christ –
Hallelujah!!
(Oh, God.)
He conjures a reality
of one more slightly hysterical
Christo-Buddhist, or perhaps
just another boodle Christian
Searching hopefully,
one supposes,
for claw marked clavicles,
devilish indentations,
and the slightest wisp
of sulfur.

His ride along, the blue
eye shadowed perky one,
twenty years past the last perk,
sits, wide-eyed, knees pressed
and molded together,
in unchanging,
perhaps unchangeable, agastness.
The game hasn't started yet,
and her cheer led team's
down by 40.
She blinks, one thinks,
at most, hourly.

The third one, a three year pastor,
is an old street fighter
gone to seed with memories
of triumphal martial arts.
He wants, needs, hopes for,
somebody, anybody,
someone else please,
to do the work
he doesn't know how to do.

> Jeez, I can hardly wait
> To meet the rest
> Of the team.

Later, sitting alone,
unblinking and deeply clawed,
not knowing what to do,
the thought wanders through
that all of it,
absolutely all of it,
is grace.

Grace

Fan was her name.
It was a week before
I realized
she spelled it P-h-a-n,
which was short for Phantasy.
She was seventeen,
blind from birth,
raised by her grandparents
outside of Las Cruces.
This was her first season
in the big city – here to learn
about buses and schedules,
and dorm rooms,
and eating out,
and how to work
with other people.
One morning in her third week,
she came early to work.
Earlier still and alone,
I was already in the place.
She came through the side door,
the door for staff and volunteers,
paused, and said to herself,
the angels present, and the unseen me,
"I just love this place!"

Close to finishing her six weeks
with us,
as tradition called for,
she was given her choice

of a going away present.
"A TV – I'm going to really need a TV."
As always in that place,
just in time and just enough,
the day before she was to leave,
someone gave us a small, portable TV.
The thing actually worked –
and worked well –
both sight and sound.
On the morning of her leave-taking,
she received her really needed TV.
That afternoon, her Grandfather
came to pick her up
for the trip back home.
He stood away from her
and only said, softly, "Phan."
She grew to somewhere
about ten feet tall
and said, "Oh Grandpa! Oh Grandpa!
you gotta see my new TV."
Ear to ear teeth, eyes going crazy,
the cane swinging like a scythe,
she went and took him
to her new and necessary TV,
turned it on and said, "Isn't that
the best TV you've ever seen?
Isn't it just the best?"

Oh, dear, sweet, unsighted one,
may God, wherever and however
you are, enfold and protect you,
and bless you as you have me,
even onto this day.

Droit de Refuser – Merci Beaucoup

for Bill Nevins

For millennia in other voices, for centuries
in our own, poesy was joined onto the structure
of the tongue. Ours and it
never were a comfortable fit.
in and over time, here, in this place,
iambs, dactyls, anapests scanned
into rhythms we did not speak.
Whitman saw the chance, the need,
and took it. Masters, Sandburg, Crane,
Hart and Stephen, and countless others
pushed out with force this new breath,
this loud and raucous, belly shaking, quaking,
new day laughter – not the languid tea cozy
covered insipid porcelain pot
of hand wringing, self referential, elitist,
bullshit we were accustomed to.
These new singers heard and taught us,
the people, a new language
and how to speak it.
We have fought and grappled
for this true melody of hearts and lungs
ever since. Howled for it even.
I will not give it up.
Neither will I dance a minuet or quadrille.
I will not, even perversely,
or as a curiosity, become a museum piece.
I am no Frog Automaton
spewing out sonnets or sestinas
on demand.

I am no keeper of ancient voice or form,
of useless seals, or unhinged gates.
"I yam what I yam!"
A small creator of small creations,
and curator of none.

Excusez moi, mon Maître.
Je ne pelle pas merde.

After Reading Nevins' Skibbereen

So..........so.........so.
We'll whisper, as befits her.
So, have you never seen a real Sheela na Gig?
Not a carved and stonish one
named by unknowing, brainless plodders
of field expeditions - but a real live,
walking and talking one,
carrying her mattress on her back?
A queen sized one at that?
And being so heavy weighted,
and she so small,
scuttling faster down a street
than you can run?
Leaving a church where she abode,
by a welded, side locked portal?
And the idiots inside – a thousand of them
beating their drums as if it
still was yesterday, and things
were hunky fine? Not knowing
the rack and ruin her absence
would bring? Have you?
Well, I have, and until tonight,
and thanks to Bill the Bard,
I never knew a name for her.
All I knew was when she left,
it was time for me to leave as well.
To this night, 20 and more years later,
she still scares the shit out of me.

The Project

Joe Williamson

Never conked his hair.
It just looked like it.
Had gone to the Army late,
Was what he said,
In WWII, and spent time
In Japan afterward.
Somewhere there
He was seen not as nigger
But as man by someone,
And maybe began to love
And then came home
To North Carolina
To the place his folks had.
One night, walking home
On a country road,
Had been passed by a carload of
Good ol' boys, who yelled
The wrong thing at him,
And gone on a ways
And then turned around,
And he knew were coming back
To kill him.
He had a small revolver
And before they had the chance,
He fired at them
Like his Uncle taught him.
They spun around
And took off,

And when he got home,
Told his mother
What he'd done,
And she said he had
To leave right then
And there
And that's how he
Got to Detroit,
Where I met him
Years later.
He taught me
How to make a living.
He was an honest man
And a good one.
He knew, before I did,
What it would mean
If I stayed crazy,
And in that particular way
He learned in North Carolina
He helped me to survive.

John Sullivan

Had "the press"
Which was high blood pressure.
He worked harder
Than any three men,
Drank more than any four,
And walked out from work,
No matter how hard the day
Or dirty the work, in wing tips

And a pork pie hat,
Sharp as a tack,
Clean as a hound's tooth.
He ran red lights
From half a block away
And laughed
For the next three blocks.
The press got him at 55,
But God, he had fun.

Boddery

Pete Boddery,
       Tough foreman.
He'd hired me when I told him
I could do the job
And didn't lie.
Twenty years before,
He worked the docks
In San Francisco
When the troop ships
Pulled out loaded
With cannon fodder
For the South Pacific
And left behind
Brand new wives
Crying in their handkerchiefs
And looking for support.
On the nights
Of those days,
Boddery said he never,

Not once even,
Slept in his own bed.
He quit seven years
After he hired me
When the first
Of the snot nosed
Butthead bean counters
Came through
Calling for a reduction
In work units,
Which meant man-hours,
Which meant somebody
Was gonna get laid off.
Old Pete said, "Screw you,
You bastards,
I'll save you the trouble."
And he quit
Instead of laying off
A man he'd hired.

My Grandson Kyle

Has a project
To write of the mentors
In his life.
Mine were the ones
Who in living
Quite ordinary lives
Allowed me to watch
And gather information
On what it takes

To be a human being.
None of them
Will make the histories
Of the times.
None would even think,
Even now,
Even if they were alive,
How extraordinary
Their integrity,
Their wholeness, was.

Oklahoma

Dear Kyle;

The dirt here is red,
mirroring perhaps
an ancestral presence
of countless families,
clans, tribes,
and gatherings.
Ancient and unnumbered,
before this counted time
of the sullen and fearful,
they reside deeply unseen
and clear as a human face.
From before this common 'era,
faces turned,
as yours does today,
from these prairies
toward stars and moons,
and suns and skies,
and seasons,
and simmering days,
and cold killing nights,
and in their turning,
and in yours,
spoken and unspoken,
asked and unasked,
the questions always
and almost forever come:
"Who?" and "Why?"
and "Me?" and "Why?"

and always the And,
almost forever.

Fate and karma
reduce us to stringless
marionettes, heaped
limb upon limb,
helpless to turn
and ask
what must be asked,
even if unanswered.
Tonight, perhaps,
or tomorrow night,
walk out to the so close
New Mexico stars,
and ask them some questions.
    They will not answer.
Ask the Manzanos some questions.
    They will not answer.
Or ask the Sandias.
or ask the sky and the clouds,
or the desert willow,
or ask the desert itself.
Neither function nor nature,
nor any other attribute,
will allow a response
to the singularity of our being,
but in your questions,
in the questing of one of us,
by and in and through
the one of us called you,
the universe will have spoken
in the remembering of the word.

Such a responsibility should,
of course,
be taken very lightly.

I love you,
Papa Bob

Failure to Thrive

The baby was, at most, eight months old.
Her new foster mother volunteered with us
and brought her in as much for what to do,
as for some kind of respite.
The baby (there is no recollection of the name)
was encased in plaster. Royal blue plaster.
A full body cast with only her face
and the tips of her fingers and toes uncased.
Her eyes were the dead eyes
of the thousand yard stare.
The other women, as always with matter of fact
and tender courage, took over.
Some women took the baby and held her
and talked to her and rocked her.
Some other women held the new mother,
and talked with her, and sat with her,
and touched her.
The baby had been beaten and broken almost from birth.
The x-rays showed the old breaks in bones now healed,
and somewhat newer breaks halfway healed,
and now the latest spiral fractures of the longest bones.
She could not move her body until the healing
was far enough along to put her in a turtle cast
to enable treatment of her skin and pressure sores.

There was a group of Christian (Baptist) kids
visiting us – about twenty-five of them.
In the mornings they would sort clothing
and help the clients with their food.
That afternoon, when most of the women

Went home, the Director asked these kids,
these teenagers, if they would hold
the encased baby and sing to her
and pray for her.
And they did quietly sing, and gently
pass her one to another, and pray over
and weep over this broken one.
They gave their thanks with one quiet,
softly sung, hymn and song after another.
And the thousand yard,
eight month stare continued.
Two hours they sang and prayed,
and I watched as one untimely born,
until there came a movement
in the eyes of the child, and then a focus
on the one singing to her.
And then the eyes shifting to another singer
and another focus on another singer,
and still another focus.
Someone brought the new mother
to the baby who could not move
and for the first time, with eyes alive,
They met, and the fingers of the little one
began to move. And the toes.
The holding of the child was passed to the mother,
who cried, one believes, sweet tears.
Two hours later, the place was empty.
The mother home in contact with her baby.
The kids back on their way to Houston.
Something had happened,
some intervention of grace abounding,
some brief miracle, perhaps of love
and compassion that would,

or would not last.

I never saw any of them again.
I only know it happened.

Detroit City

James Johnson Junior, in the Great Magnolia State
of Mississippi, had seen
with his nine year old eyes, his cousin's lynched
and dead, and mutilated body.
Twenty-six years later,
at the Chrysler Eldon Avenue Plant,
in Detroit, on July 15, 1970,
James Johnson Junior killed
two white shirted foremen,
one white, and one black,
and one job setter,
with an M1-30 caliber carbine,
loaded with years of harassment,
and put downs, and downed hopes,
and threats, and being laughed at.
The bosses fired him at the start of shift.
James went home and got the carbine
and a second badge
to get him back into the plant,
back to the hotter than hell furnaces,
where they'd tried to make him
work that morning.
At his trial for murdering three men,
James Johnson Junior
was found not guilty (innocent)
by reason of insanity,
by a jury of his peers,
who visited the Eldon Plant,
and decided that
the Chrysler Motor Car Company,

the incarnation of faceless,
therefore blameless evil,
had driven James Johnson Junior
murderously insane.
He spent 5 years in the Ionia State Hospital,
where he sued Chrysler for workmen's comp
and won.
They had to pay him seventy five dollars a week,
not because he killed three people,
but because the conditions,
the horror, the inhumanity,

The heat, the meanness,
the speedups, the white supremacy,
those things Chrysler truly employed,
and were its most loyal and true employees,
had turned James Johnson Junior
into a killer of men.

Chrysler closed the Eldon plant.
The weed choked parking lots added
to the NoTown MoTown emptying of Detroit.
But after that day in July of 1970,
the foremen and the supervisors
never again wore white shirts
and shiny shoes.

The Revolution Was Televised

And everybody thought
It was things as normal going on.
They gave it to you right out front.
A decade plus of politics by assassination.
Stupid assholes getting and staying high,
As if nothing mattered
'Cept what was goin' on
Inside their Maggot Brains.
Nixon waving goodbye. Ford coming in
With Rockefeller trailing Attica,
But nobody remembers that
Or gives a shit,
And everything's hunky dory,
And everything's hunky dory,
And everything's hunky dory,
'Cause that's what the papers
(When folks still could read)
Said.
And LA burnin' down
And Detroit and Newark.
And television said
Everything's hunky dory,
Not to worry,
Everything's hunky dory,
And MTV, and a thousand damn
Bullshit channels never runnin' outa bullshit.
And Reagan, killin' the unions,
And El Salvador, and Granada,
And Panama, and Guatemala,
And Honduras, and Bolivia,

And all the other places,
And even Pine and Ruby Ridge,
Goddamit!
And Charlie Wilson's War
That never ended,
And everything's hunky dory,
And everything's hunky dory,
And everything's hunky dory,
And Iraq doubled down,
And Somalia, Kosovo,
Rwanda, the undeclared Congo
Again and again,
And the smallpox blankets never stopped.
This time the IMF passed out
Structural Realignment
Where babies got killed
By the bottom line,
And the interest rates in '80,
And everything's hunky dory.
And everything's hunky dory,
And everything's hunky dory.
Liberia for Christ's sake!
Blood and more blood.
Now folks are finally gettin'
The idea they ain't shit.
And it's way too late.
Go ahead, sucker,
And lay your life down —
See what don't happen —
When nobody gives a shit,
And everything's hunky dory.

The Second Burrito

Late of a chilled October
Saturday morning,
ducked under heavy covers,
my wife massages my shoulder
and says it's time to get up.
The foundling dog we just found
to be pregnant jumps
on the bed to nuzzle,
and in some fashion
of dog thought or feeling,
seeks to be safe and wanted,
which she is.
Later in the big room,
a misplaced and out of season
CD begins to call upon angels
to harken and sing whatever angels
sing unto the newborn King.
Halfway through the second burrito,
from nowhere,
It occurs that Afghanistan
scans iamb. Iraq as well scans
the great iamb.
And then come thoughts
of poppy and killing fields
and heroin routes and tracks,
and an old dead friend
who was a member of Delta
before there was a Delta Force,
who was sent too many times

Into Vietnam, and Laos,
and South America,
to kill selected and specific targets.
He said, one day, that war was a machine,
and that the machine had to be kept working,
and that it had to be oiled and lubricated
with human blood,
and that the tools of war, like food
on supermarket shelves,
had to be consumed, restocked,
and rotated, so the oil and grease
for the machine
would always be fresh.
Three weeks before he died,
I held him down
on his hospital bed,
while he flashed back,
screaming and thrashing,
to a firefight where some guy
named Leo was bleeding out.
An hour after my old friend died,
I held his cooling head
in my hands and gave thanks
for his new safety,
        safe from the screaming
and thrashing,
        from the re-re-remembered
killing and dying,
        safe from Leo,
safe from the haunting and uncounted
faceless bleeding ones dying out again.

The passage passes.
The CD angels unharkened
no longer sing.
The half-eaten burrito
goes into the garbage.
The dog and I go for a walk
into the ghost chasing
chilled October wind.

Sonny

In the very early days,
he'd been a contract writer.
And if he'd done what he was supposed
to do when he was supposed to do it,
nobody ever would have heard of Marvin Gaye.
Instead he married another writer,
had two kids, got divorced, and another job,
and sang with his sister Mary
who played piano, and his brother Al
who played bass, in the afternoons,
after work, in the front room
of their Mother's three family flat,
with first floor French windows that opened
to a small porch and a ghetto yard filled
on warm summer afternoons and nights
all the way across the street, with people
who came to hear, through those windows,
the best music they would hear in years
or maybe ever.
          Late of an afternoon,
I was trying to get through the crowd,
up the stairs, and a guy asked me
what the fuck I was doing,
and Sonny stuck his head
out the window, and said,
"He lives here." From then on,
there were no problems,
and young Whitey X rolled on through
like Moses at the Red Sea.

Now, forty-five years later,
Mary dead twenty-plus years
from cancer, and Al about to die,
Sonny and I talk on the phone
every couple of months -
two old men with the gimps
old men have, with the distances
of time and the heartbeats
only survivors can claim.
He wakes, as I do, each morning,

With the thought, the hope,
that while this ain't heaven,
it sure as hell ain't hell.

And somehow, again,
if only in these memories,
Sister Mary's left foot is again shoeless,
and her bare heel is stomping the beat
on the wooden floor, hard and strong,
and powerful, and Brother Al
is playing bass with his controlled
and contented four string mania,
and Sonny is singing from a heart so big
it makes grown men almost cry
at the beauty of it. And I am still
the watching ghetto white kid
too crazy to mess with.
And a whole world, a whole world,
is filled with joy, the joy,
the joy and the beauty of every single
moment of that time.
And there ain't a god damned thing wrong

with a crazy old man
for the membrance of that memory.

Canzone della Creazione

So beautifully simple.
The curve of the question not needing an answer.
The lightness of light in her eyes.
Light shimmering with joy upon her hair.
Even the grass, the buds,
even the trees, the clouds, the air,
even the colors, all colors seen and unseen,
bend toward her beauty.
She dances with no weight of gravity.
Her grace is boundless.
Her movements flow from a source without name
and bring peace to all that surround her.
She is the island of an expanding universe
where light glows and grows from light,
where the sound of her breathing gives birth to mercy,
where her arms give sweep to stars and galaxies,
where all is her lightness and goodness and wonder.
Around her is no elaboration,
only the substance and heart of the real,
as free as fire, as solid as the wind,
as transparent as the freshet her warming hand
turns into the ripple and roar of truest laughter.
All things turn to face her face.
Her eyes require the end of care and sorrow.
Her steps across time and space
leave only the surety of her presence.
She is beyond measure, beyond the touch of texture.
Beyond our reach, she reaches out to join us.
The mist to rain, the rain to mist. And rain again.
And light and darkness circling forever.

All around her are the circles of life
harmonized within her love.
No storm gathers in her presence
save to be loved into and out of existence.
No hatred continues without absorption
or final extinction within her gaze.
No single cry of hurt or joy goes unheard.
Each tear shed is shed and shared by her as well.
Every giggle, every ounce of laughter
is rolled on floors, walls, and ceilings
and is met there where she is best and most herself
in toothless grins of small and old,
of those whose breathing and breathless time
has come somehow into her place
of comfort and peace and joy.
She is unknown and unknowable,
and familiar and fully known.
She hides nothing, fears nothing,
and still knows the hidden no-thing,
and the gossamer thin thread of fear.
She walks gently as the softest summer breeze,
and still her tread shakes mountains.
She feeds all things freely from her body.
Within her, all is melody, and all is harmony.
Within her, the lion and the lamb are one.
Within her, all are songs of joy and wonder.
Within her, all is the song of creation.

Finally

The fault, the fault, the fault.
All of the fault was mine.
I made things happen. I don't know why.
But it was always my fault. For years my fault.
Then came the booze, the stuff.
The anger and fights. The red hot hate -
The purest thing going.
Early on, I knew what you would do
before you did or said it.
It was the way you looked
at what you looked at –
at what you saw that I saw in you,
that all of you were bastards.
Then came Fuck Fault, just control.
Control. And more control.
It was not the knife that did it –
Only the sharp edged threat.
You touch me again, and I'll kill you.
At eleven, I knew where to stick you –
Up through the solar plexus
and into the diaphragm,
and then watch you try to breathe.
Later came the wasted years,
the hatred well disguised,
so, so, so socially acceptable,
such worthy, worthwhile activities,
causes without fault,
and for years and years
underneath, and deep, deep down,
the hatred of it all.

The night before she died,
my mother called to say she loved me.
She'd died long before that night
when I knew she knew.

In my thirty-fourth year,
in a Houston airport restaurant
with an uncle, unseen for decades,
who says so quietly, over pancakes,
"It's a miracle you survived."
As quietly, I ask, "You knew?"
"We all knew," he said.
"You knew what they did to me?"
His eyes began to change,
to blink, and blink again.
A silence, still and oh so silent,
whispered at last,
"We all knew, Bobby."

Jesus, how clear it came,
back from the months I lived among them,
why they carried this scent of fear,
this permeation of cowardice,
whenever I came near.
The rage was still so full, and foul,
and fire hot, so filled with death,
perhaps they knew and saw in me
their last and dying breath.

I would forgive them only for the sport of it,
the ease of it, and simply because they're dead.
If by some miracle of chance or value,

they were brought to life,
to live again in front of me,
I would cause them to breathe deeply
and eat the bloodied rotten dirt
they now have all become.

Let them forgive themselves.
My time is less than theirs
for such a thing.

Dree at 6

A normal evening - job talk
is over with dinner.
Barb bathes and sews. I read.
A grandchild calls to inform
her most loyal subject
that upon this day
she read and wrote,
and ate two kinds
of vegetables,
and some healthy fruit,
and further, that she did not play,
that this day she was not
"A play kind of person."
We talk and she struggles
with my age and hers.
Perhaps the difficulty of now
and then, of here
and there, of used
to be and not now,
is clearest on the cleanest slate.
She reaches forward to me
not knowing
that for me she must reach back.
The struggle is momentary.
We accept what is as is.
This wondrous child,
this aging coot,
this thrice blessed day
of serious vegetables
and healthy fruit.

A prayer prayed over Robert Bruce Morrison (March 15, 1964 –
May 4, 2002) 40 days after his birth, at the Churching of his mother.
From The Book of Common Prayer, 1928, page 307.

Then May Be Said:

Grant,
> *Give and make possible*

We beseech Thee
> *Asking and imploring*

Oh Heavenly Father
> *Giver of all*

That the child
> *This wondrous one,*
> *This Robert Bruce,*
> *Held close*
> *And come early*

Of this Thy servant
> *This present one*
> *This Barbara, mother,*
> *In tears and travail*

May daily increase
> *Grow large and strong*

In wisdom
> *The knowledge*
> *Of your love*

And stature
> *The shape*
> *Of your love*

And grow
> *Be stretched*

And empowered

In Thy love
> *Your surrounding*
> *Presence*

And service
> *The duty of love*

Until he come
> *Arrive*

To Thy eternal joy
> *Where he be now*

Through Jesus Christ, our Lord,
> *Servant*
> *Foot washer*
> *Saviour*
> *Friend*

Amen.
> *So be it.*

The so be it
Has now become
The so it was.
Robbie was born,
And in accordance
With this prayer
Prayed over him,
He grew daily
In ways we do not know.
The private actions
Of the Godhead
With a dedicated child
Are only to be wondered at.
He grew strong and graceful
And was fierce in winning,
Careful with the young,

And gentle with his mother.
He married, fathered children,
Was stubborn and unyielding,
And walked unnaturally
Toward the fires
That we run from.

He was caught
Inside a rat trap building
Trying to save another
As he had saved others.
In coming, full course,
From birth to blessing,
To that date, that place,
That embolism of change,
The call for help,
The going in and dying,
He came to, turned to,
Perhaps into, some infinite
Kind of grace of love,
Where wifely tears, sister sobs,
Brothers, mothers' cries
Are horribly absorbed
And given meaning
In heartstuff voice
And memory.

The killing of him twice was tried.
First by fire, then by throng.
The hero making apparat swung to,
Got legs, geared up, and handled him.
The hydra gathered its ten thousand eyes,
Counseled, decided, and excluded

Him to "hero",
Him to "the other,"
Him to the "not us,"
Him to the Olympian tribute
Of the serpentine lines
Of separation.
Quiet as a secret,
He was not "the other."
He was not some shield carried
Homeric grunt, crazed
By Athena, or tweaked
By differentiating Zeus.
He was and is, the us.
But if hero, let him be
Familial Hebrew,
Perhaps PWT,
Loving and beloved,
Husband, father, son, and brother,
Tribal, even clannish,
Excluding, not excluded,
And carefully loving.
And if there be greatness,
Let it be common,
Communal, and in love.

There can be for me
No claim of geniture,
No responsibility of blood.
Only this small part –
That for me, he was
A child of my heart,
And a dear, sweet boy and man,
Prayed over in hope at birth,

With pride in manhood,
And now, so much older now,
In grief and boundless gratitude.
Thank you, dearest of souls,
For marking my life
With your love.

Here endeth the reading.

Laura Farris

(January 9,1959- October 25, 2011)

I.

This could, but cannot be,
a love poem
of the old and usual kind.
It is forty years I have been
a bystander, watching the blooming,
The blossoming, the becoming,
of the wonder of you.
Similes and metaphors,
artifacts of imprecision,
are useless with you.
Such things point to style,
not substance. They speak
of the shine, the shimmer,
the glint of gold –
not the gold itself.
Your style and substance
cannot be extracted
one from the other.
Your goodness is just that –
            - purely and simply,
            - without alloy or addition,
                  goodness.
Your compassion is without stillness.
It works without waiting for someone else
to do the caring, the hugging, the feeding.
I could pile rock

upon rock, build cairn
after cairn, each rock a name,
each cairn a signpost
on some horizon of hope.
Each would speak
of the empty bellies you've filled,
the coats and the blankets
and the bills and rent paid
for crack babies and cracked up
mothers.
Each would speak of the hearts
you've held with such tenderness,
and the outsiders you've brought in
closer to the warmth of your love.
In the cruelest of worlds,
it would be cruelest of all
not to be loved by you.
For the ones who never said it,
and the ones who never knew how,
and the lepers who never came back,
thank you, dearest of souls,
for loving us all.

2.

There is no elegy, no eulogy,
no stringing of words – none at all –
written or unwritten, spoken or unspoken,
that could sum the fullness of this dear soul.
No words, no thoughts, no ideas,
No images, no descriptions,

could escape in truth
this emptiness, this no-thing-ness,
her death has brought.
Her mother and I wait,
in the evening of our lives
for the sweetness she would bring
to morning prayers, and we mourn
in silence and tears, unable to summon,
the words to ease this present darkness.

Why is she now breathless, and I still breathe?
Why is she now sightless, and I still see?
Why do I think, feel, taste, laugh, cry,
and bear the hollowness of useless choices,
while she has been, here and now,
reduced to memory and ashes?

She knows no longer the pain
and suffering of her last months,
but there are here now, the keepers
of these hurting, hurtful, rage filled tears,
this conjoined text of withheld, unknown,
now unknowable, years.

So – there will be no singing
of remembrances – no singing at all.
No telling of memories –
no speaking at all.
Only the sound of breathing, rasping,
in and out and out and in,
until the welcomed breathless time,
until the closing of the useless eyes,

until the final stilling of this speechless tongue,
and the quitting, the final quitting, of this pain.

3.   The Last Night

The softness of the 2:00AM wakening
and dreaming still,
the warmth of eider thoughts
and PTS Delights.
No New Yorker punditry or archiness.
No cuteness of some idiot
iteration of Billy Collins.
Only the goodness of the moment
here and now, there and then.
Last night's laughter –
Loud and quiet –
Smiles and hoohas,
and the sweet remembrance
of the daughter's sweetness,
the brilliance of her smile.
From deep in the pillow
come the memories of first times –
the first girl, the first party,
the first march, the first job,
the first time being called sir,
the first smile in my wife's voice,
the first tear wiped, the first child fed,
the first lie.
　　　　Then last times –
The last time seeing this or that one
where he should be,

closed lid and no escape.
The last look at Detroit,
or LA, or Atlanta, or Houston
out an airplane window
on a night flight
to God knows where.
The last sights, the last light,
and the faces of faces
of thousands of hungry faces
blurred tonight
into a murmuring
of voices, of backlit eyes,
and hands,
not palsied but shaking,
smooth and rough, and hard
and soft, and stretched,
racked almost to breaking
with, Help us Mister,
      Help us Mister.
Please help us.
        And from somewhere,
out of nowhere,
deeper than the pillow,
comes the winding cloth,
the enclosure, the final quiet
of the soft Egyptian cotton,
and within this moment,
not distant from it,
only present in it,
is the goodness of it all.
The horrifying, selfish,
goodness of it all.

Father's Day

Perhaps we are returned
bereft of substance,
empty or emptied,
a can or bottle
by the side of the road,
the packaging of interest
only to old men
with some sort of need
and time on their hands.
Or perhaps it is our time,
some history of the lost,
that is the measure
of our being found.
Or perhaps being filled
and emptied and found
are only passing conceits
of hope,
like the tone
before dialing
a wrong number,
or waiting
for a phone call
or a visit
that will never come again.

The Lie

This morning, the phone rang.
            Sleep settled eyes misread
            the caller ID, and I answered it.

The wrong person was there.

A week and a half,
from Maryland to Oregon,
we have been praying for his child,
his 8 year old, his daughter,
his precious and shining one,
in a coma, her hands
and feet at risk of amputation.
Another minister had called
and asked for prayer.
            Until this morning, we had not talked
            together for most of a year,
            before that at least twice a week.

            We have been separated by more
            than distance and phone bills.

He began to speak of the situation,
 of the Website they have constructed
 for changing news of her and then says,
            There has been some improvement.

            I ask if he's eating and maintaining
himself for the long haul.
As much as possible, he says.

When I ask how he is,
he begins to cry, to sob.

In the quieting down, the breathing
deeply of grief and fear, he asks,
almost strangling on the word,
        "Why?" Again, some seconds later,
        clearer, whispering, "Why?"

I will not remind him of what we know.
Remembered truth is bullshit here.

The necessary, sacred, holy
"I don't know" lie is spoken.
For us in this place,
there are no inadvertent crosses.
We know the why,
the why knows us.
The how come has now
become the how.

It almost always works.
In the middle of the night,
alone,
        and something occurs,
some recall of hope,
something that says,
this is not
all there is —
some other luminosity,
a half-sure certainty
that yes, shit happens.

And yes, grace abounds.
And yes, things fall apart.
And yes, grace abounds.
And yes, sensible is nonsense.

That yes is the only way
to stay true; yes.
> Yes to thank you for the caring,
> the grace, the compassion,
> for the love and trust
> and laughter and blessing.

Thank you
for the possibility of yes.

It almost always works.

About the Author

Bob Warren is without credentials of any kind. He never graduated from anything, never received a diploma or certificate of completion from any sort of institution of either higher or lower learning.

At the age of thirteen, he stole all of his school records and spent that school year teaching himself at the Detroit Institute of Arts. He quit school at fifteen. At seventeen, he took part in his first civil rights march. At twenty-one, he was elected Unit Steward for the Operating Engineers.

Two decades later in Houston, he went to work at a poverty church. His jobs were to lead morning prayers and to beg food for 125 to 150 families a week. He was for nine years the Associate Director for the Albuquerque Storehouse. Subsequent to that, he was Resource Director for Habitat for Humanity in Valencia County.

He is married to Barbara Warren who came to the marriage with five kids who have somehow become 19 grandkids and 18 great-grandkids.

Acknowledgements

to those who have turned hopes into realities...

First:
The Families – The Lovers

The Scott Morrison Clan ---- The David Farris Clan ----
The Peter Morrison Clan
The Laura Morrison Clan ---- The James Morrison Clan ----
The Richard Farris Clan

Second:
The Writers – The Great Hearts

Bill Nevins for kick starting it all
Lisa Gill for her courage and laughter and grace
Mitch Rayes for his kindnesses
Patricia Gillikin for never leaving anyone behind
Katrina K Guarascio for turning a sow's ear into a silk purse

Third:
The Medicos – Who Have Kept Me Alive

Mark Unverzagt -- First and foremost The Healer
Mary Alice Cooper – Who amazes everyone
Gopal Reddy – Who got blood to my brain
John Batty, Luis Constantin, and Jane Schauer -- Heart docs
with true caring hearts
Ashok Reddy and Molly Ritsema – For My Eyes

Fourth:
The Divines – Ordained and Not

Fred and Helen Holliday
Grover and Nancy Newman
Sara Armstrong and Rusty Edmundson
Harry Riser
Mike Brannon
Harold Trott
Louis Higgs
Carolyn Hughes

Val Garoza, Alexa Wheeler, Jonathan Sims – the visual ones who laugh.

Also available from

Swimming with Elephants Publications, LLC

Some of it is Muscle
Zachary Kluckman

Observable Acts
Kevin Barger

September
Katrina K Guarascio & Gina Marselle

Verbrennen
Matthew Brown

Loved Always Tomorrow
Emily Bjustrom

Of Small Children and/Other Poor Swimmers
Brian Hendrickson

To Anyone Who has Ever Loved a Writer
Nika Ann

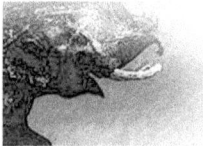

Find more titles at swimmingwithelephants.com

www.ingramcontent.com/pod-product-compliance
Lightning Source LLC
Chambersburg PA
CBHW071857020426
42331CB00010B/2552